Taking Initiative

A Continuation of
The Human Canvas Initiative
Colouring Book

Matti McLean

THE TESTER PAGE

Whether it's markers, crayons or paint use this page to test them out! Markers and ink based items are known to bleed through papers!

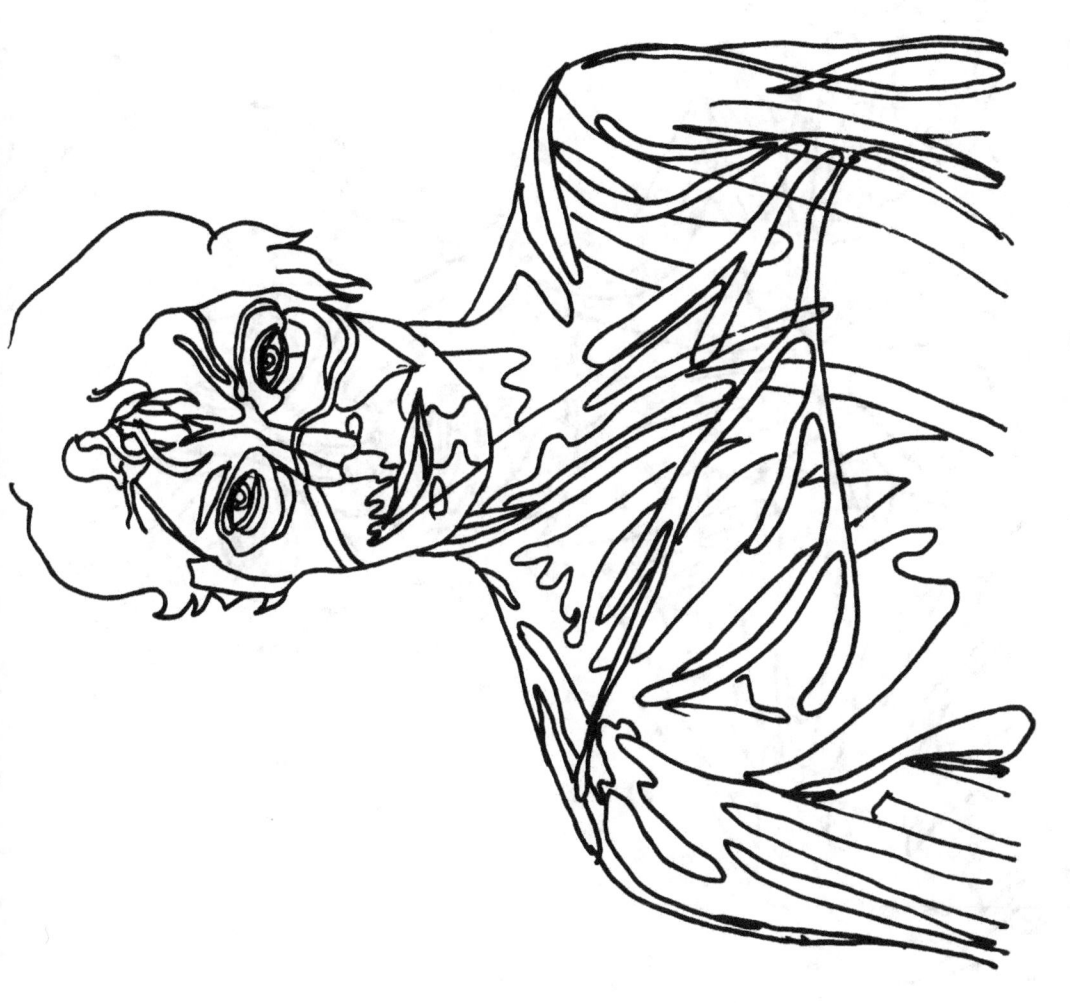

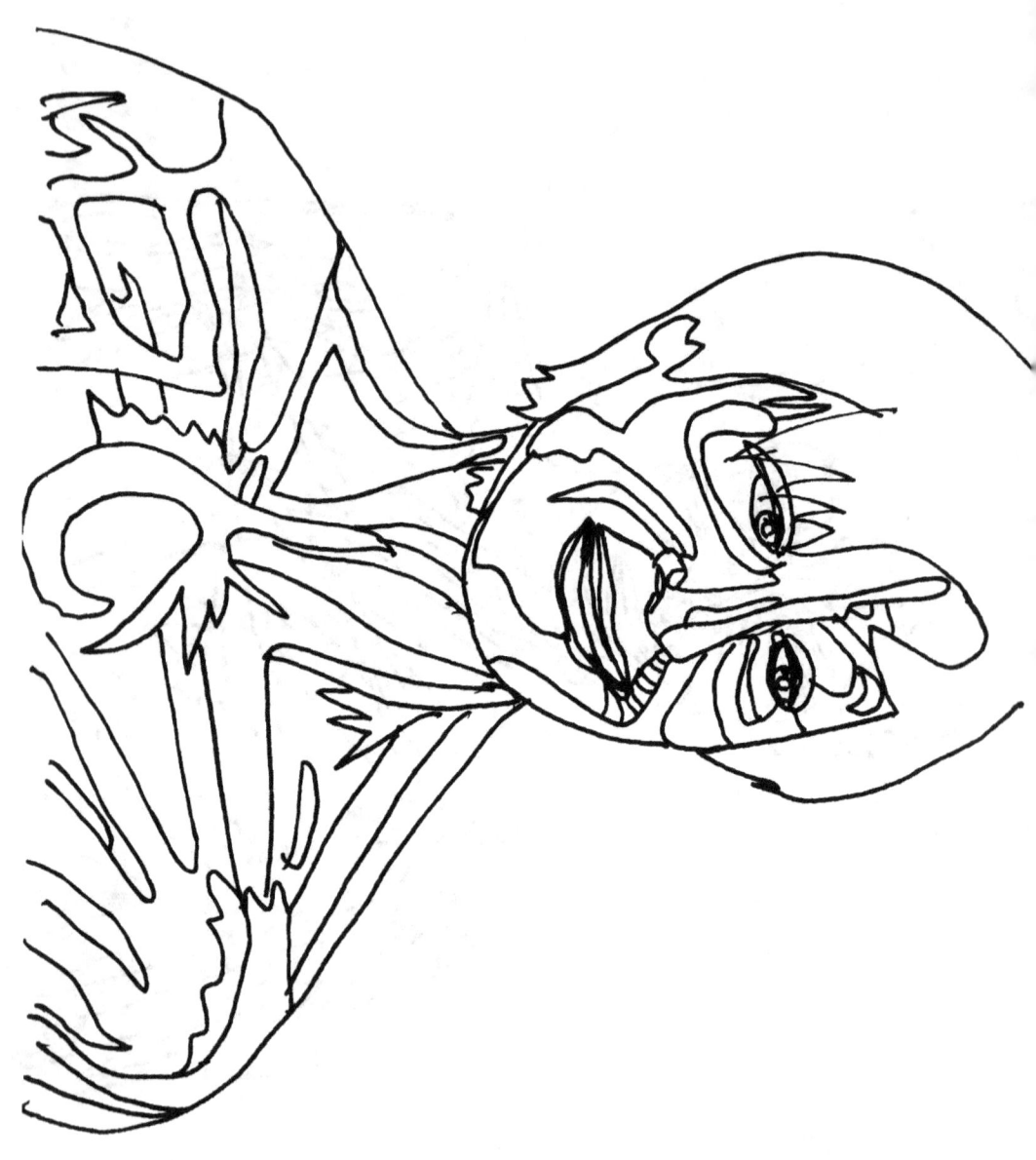

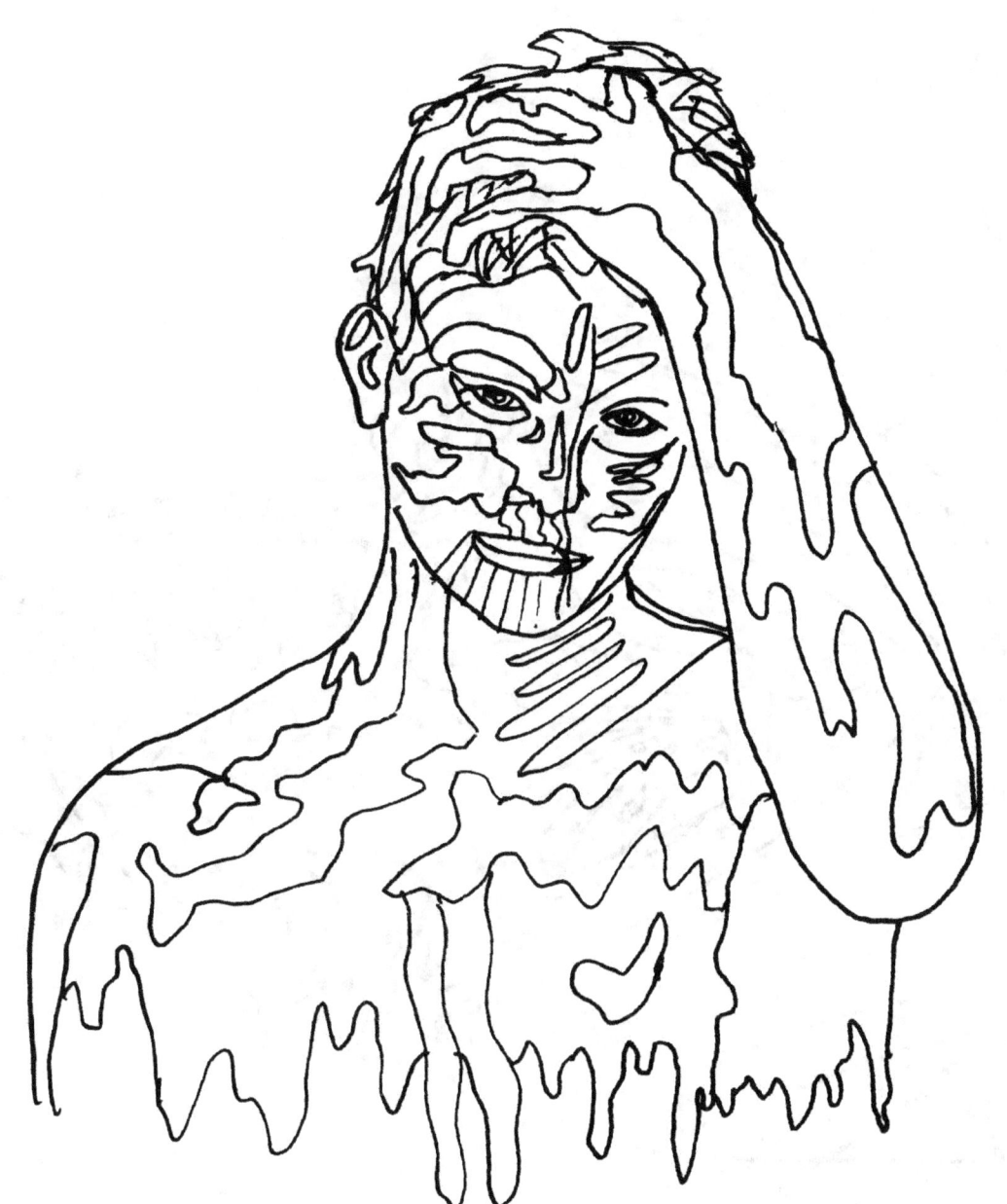

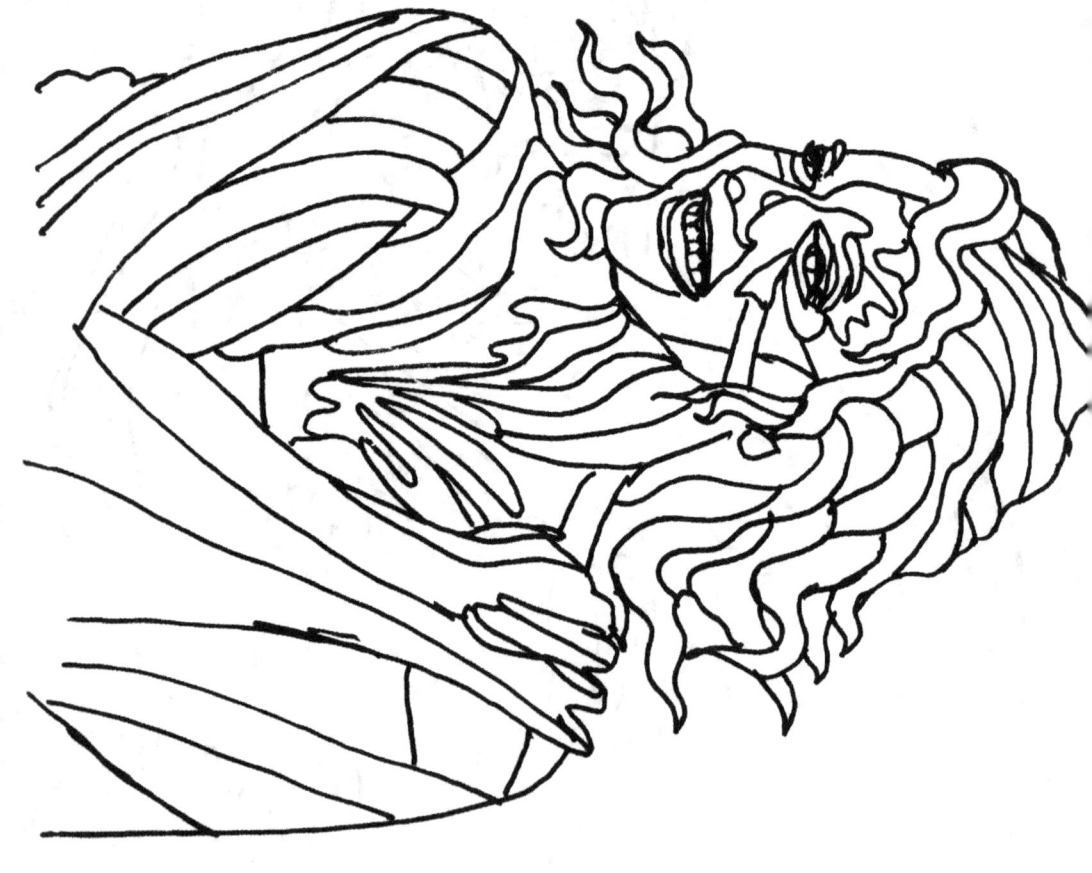

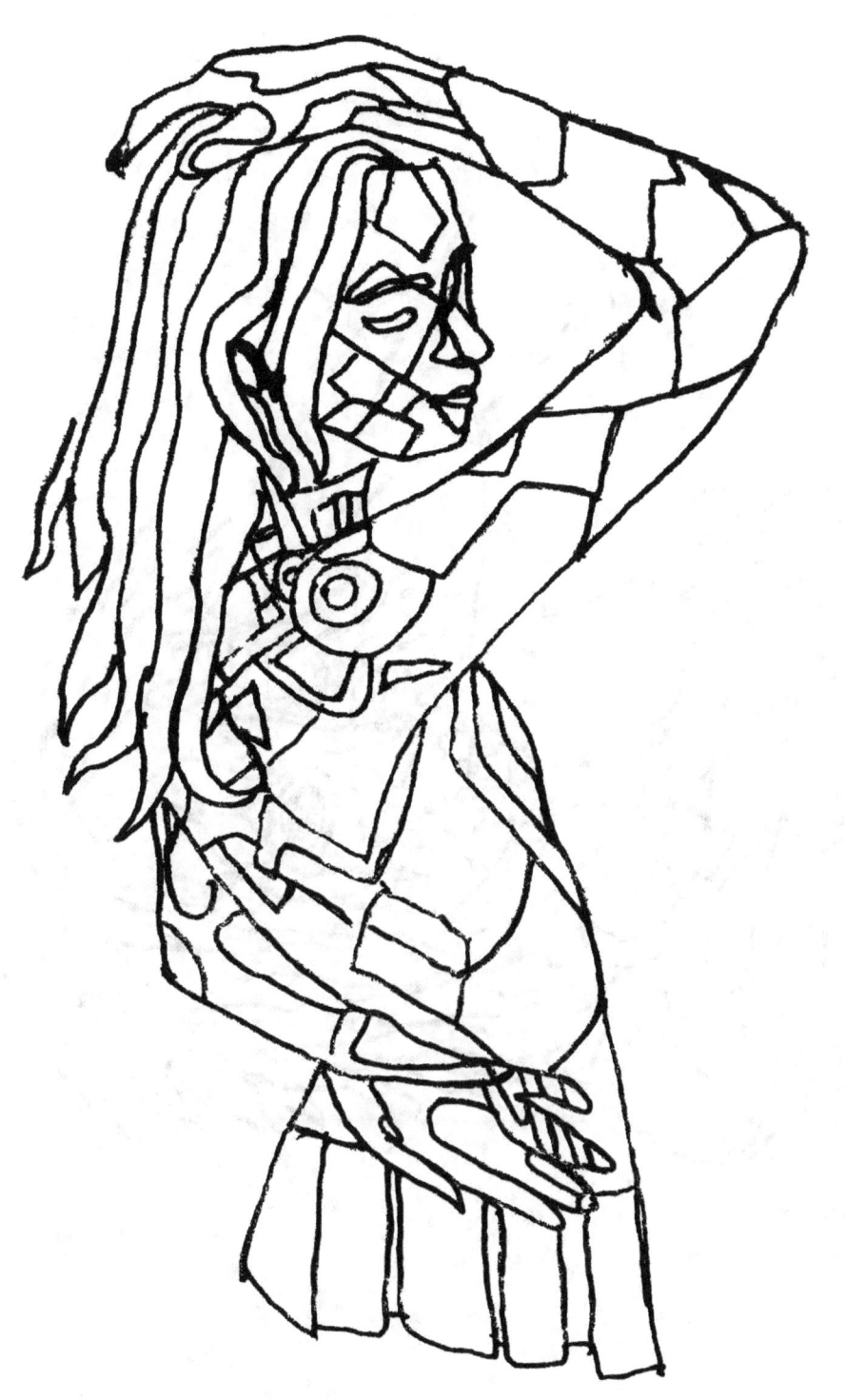

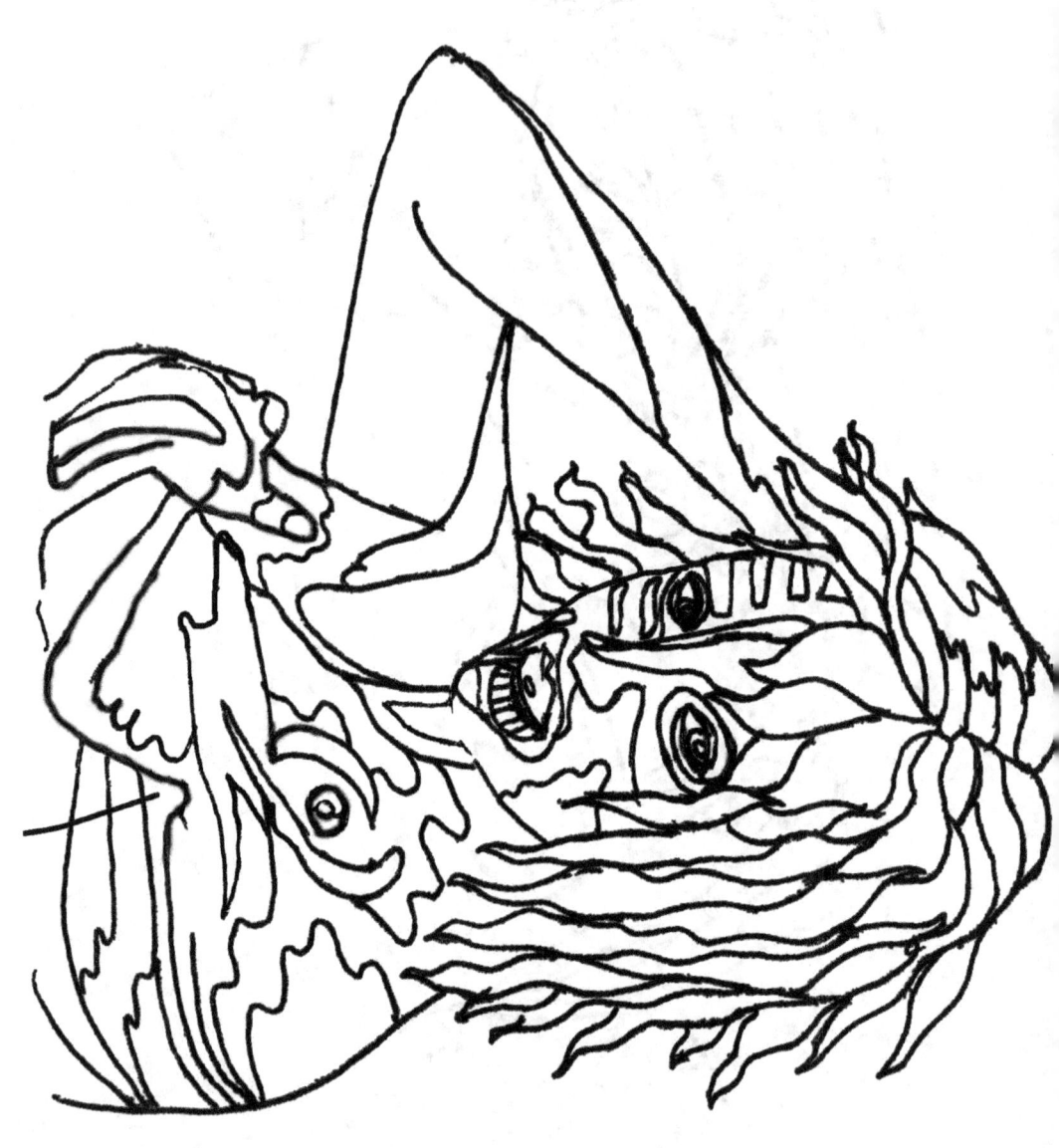

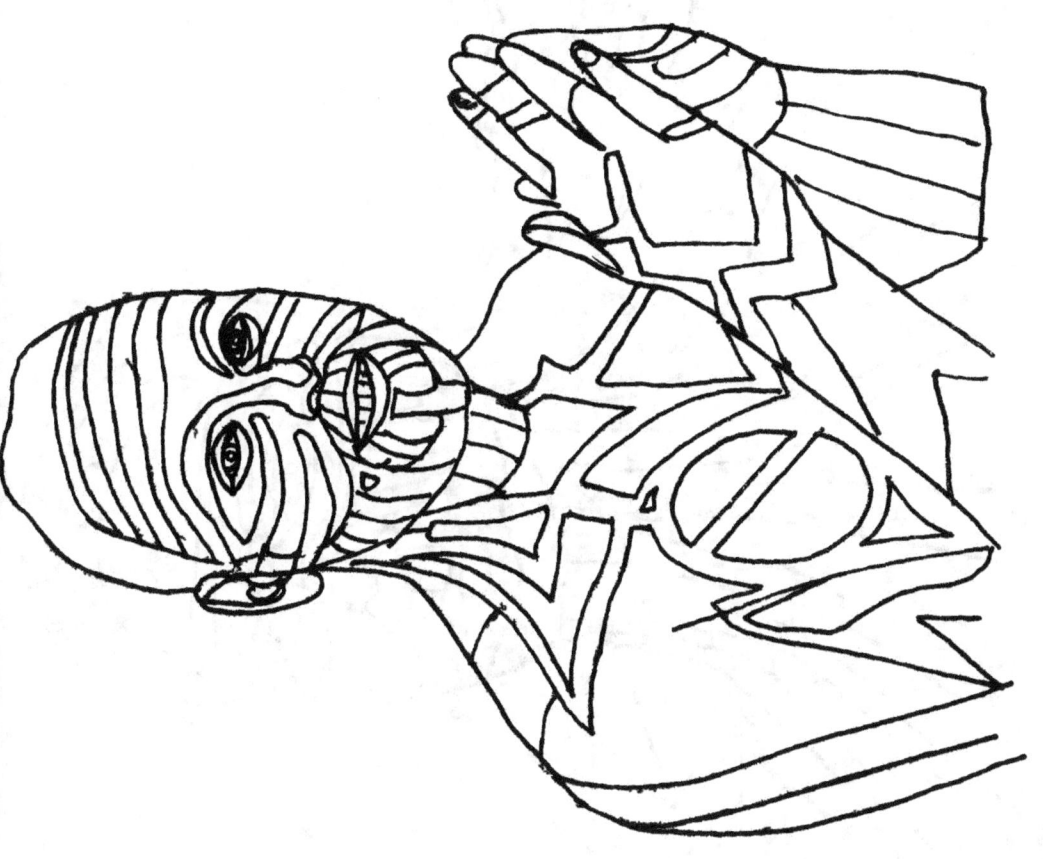

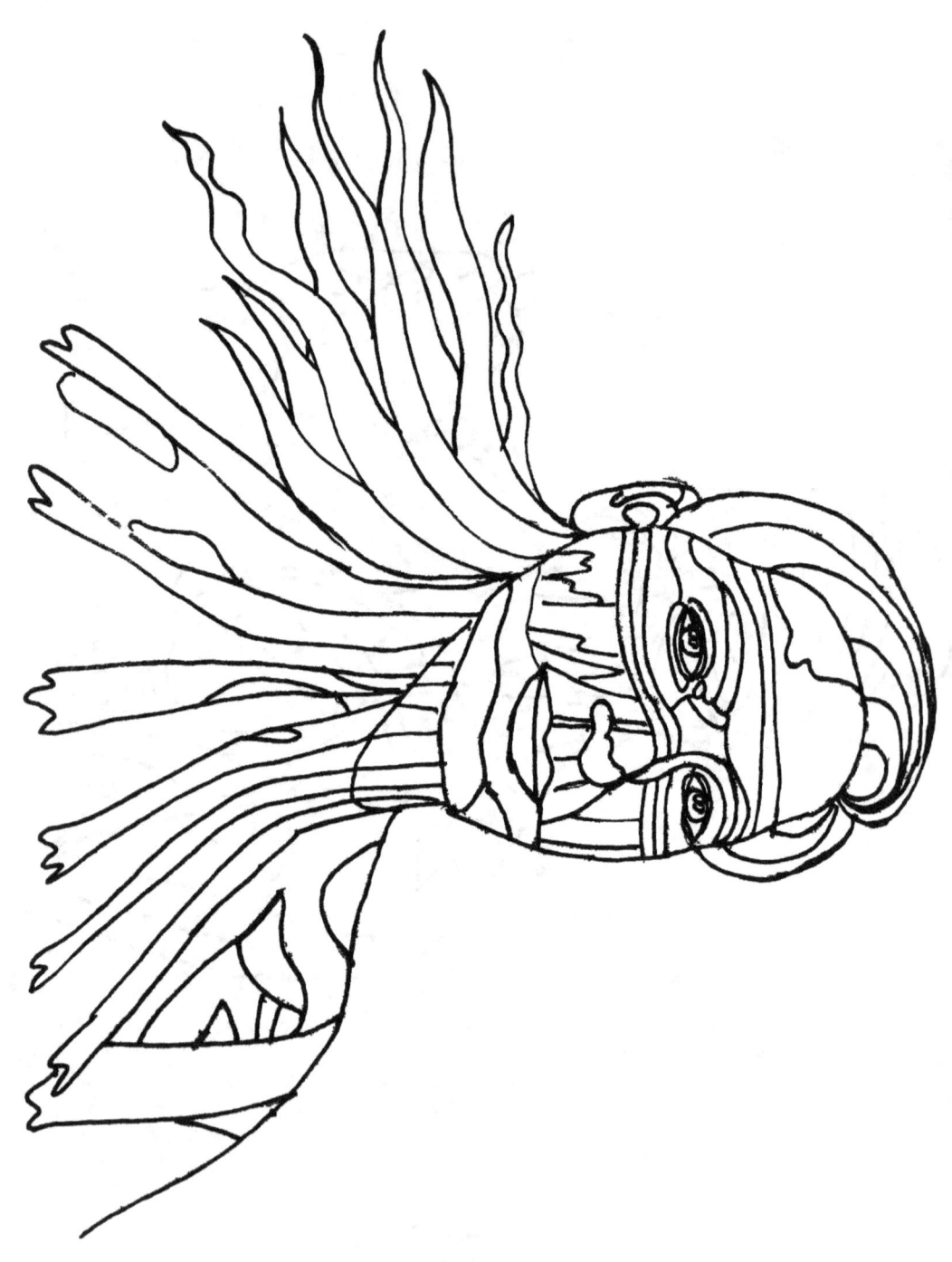

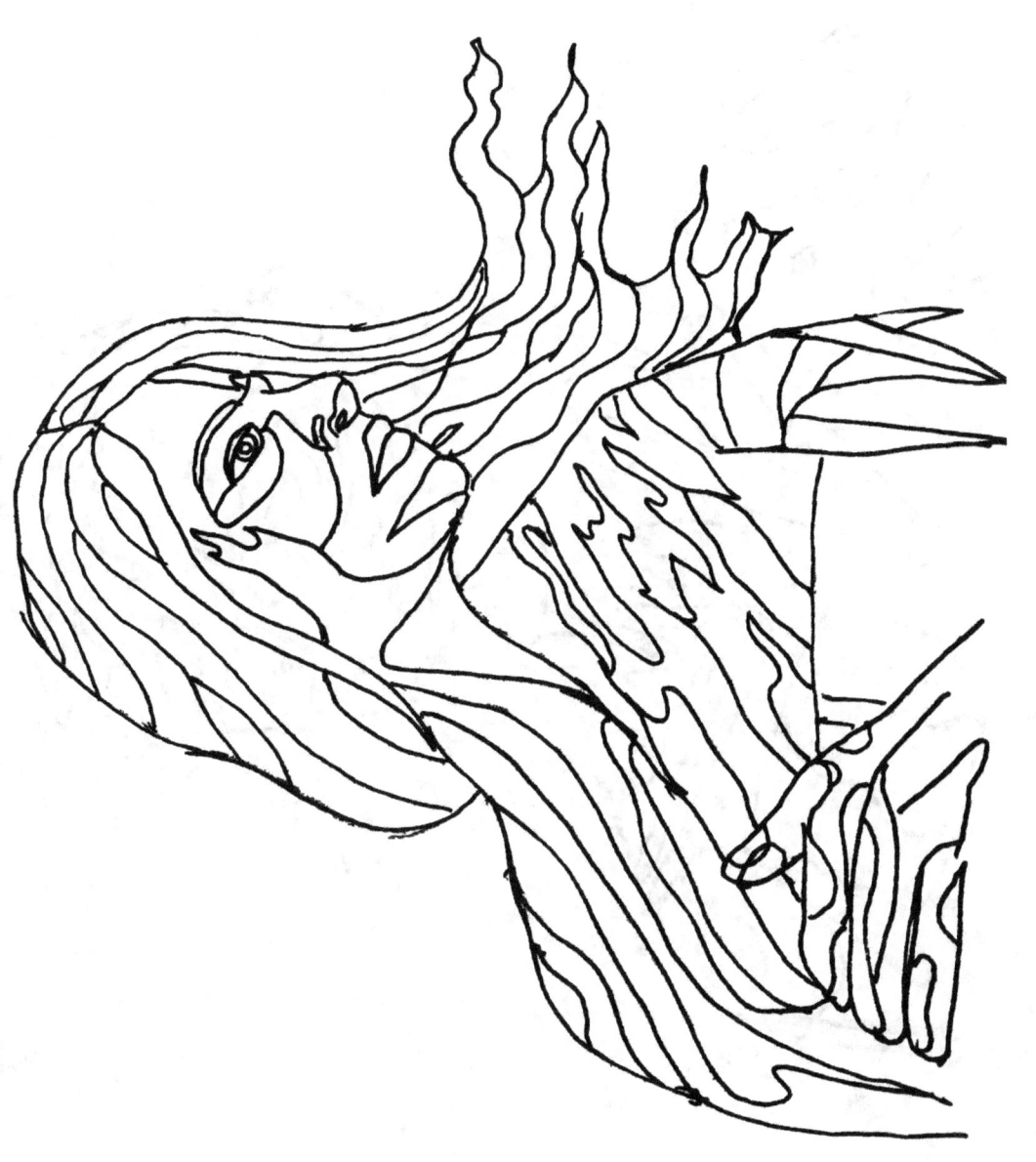

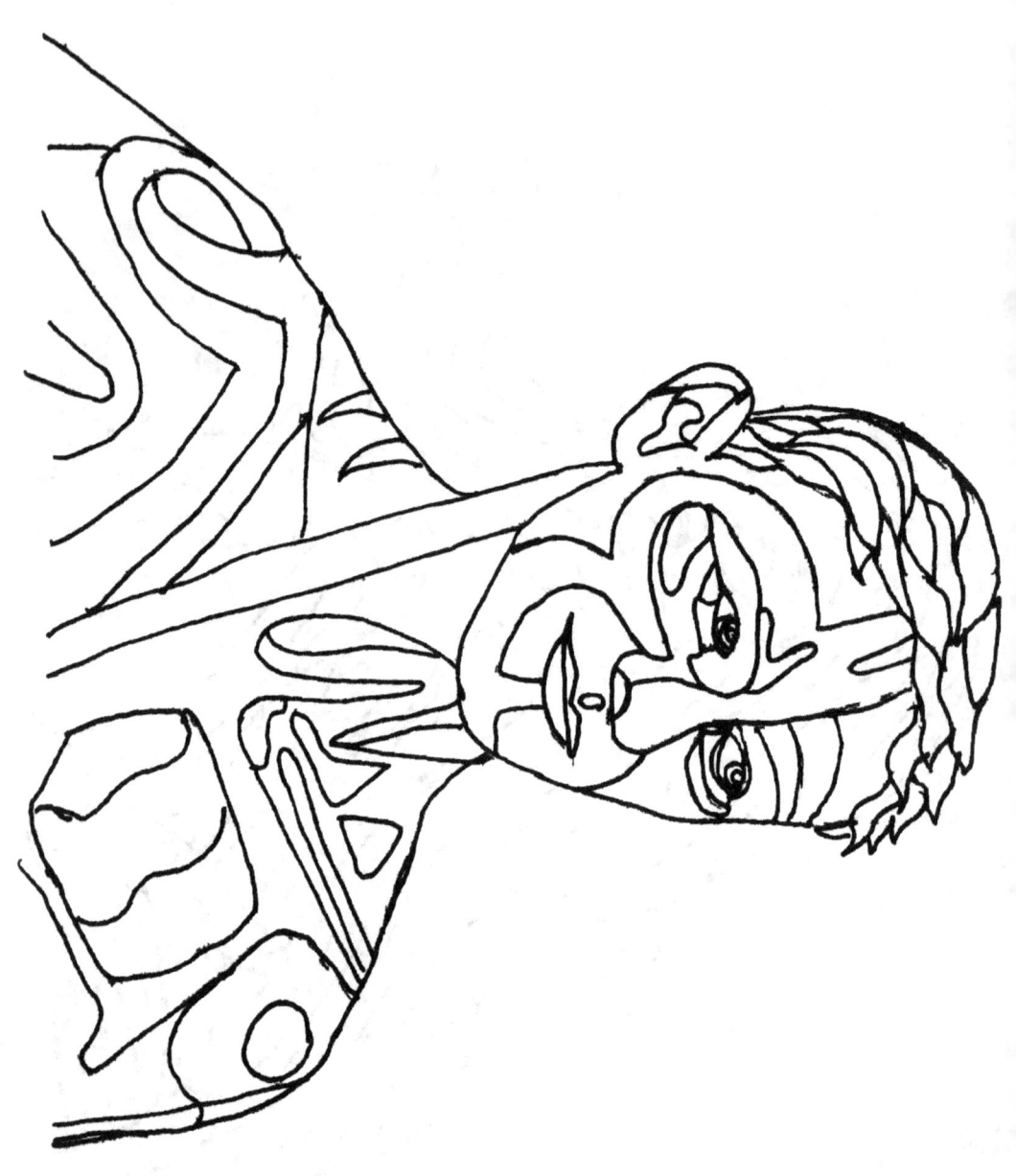

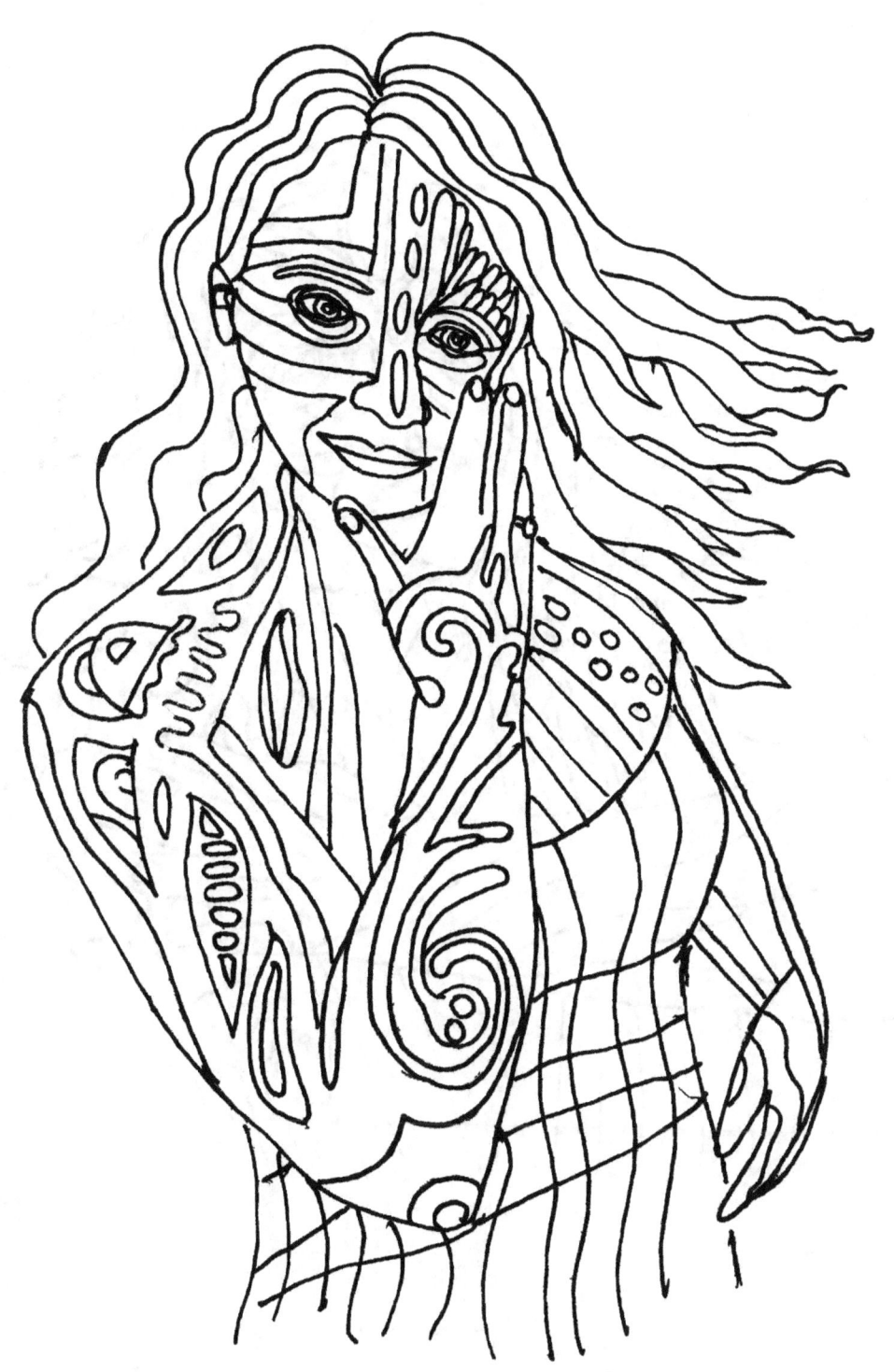

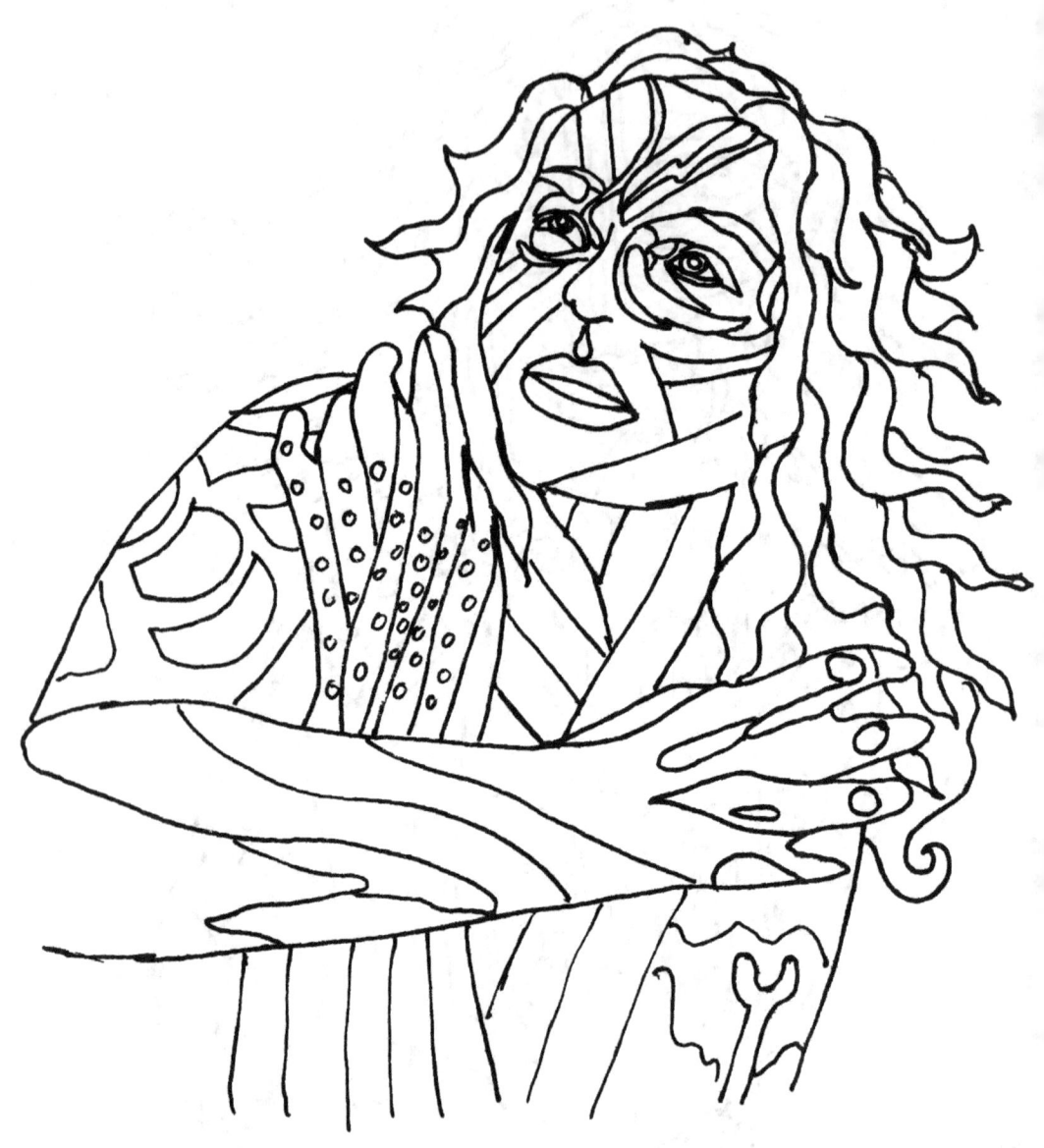

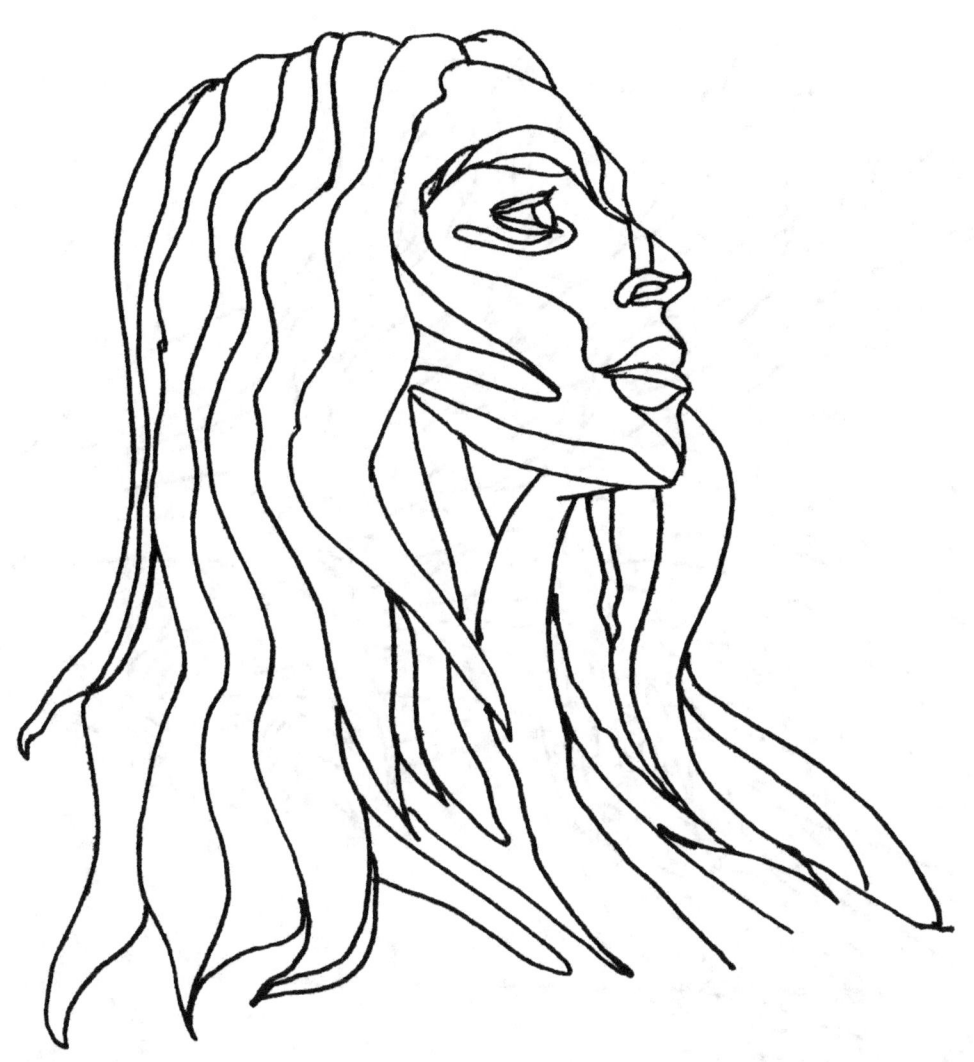

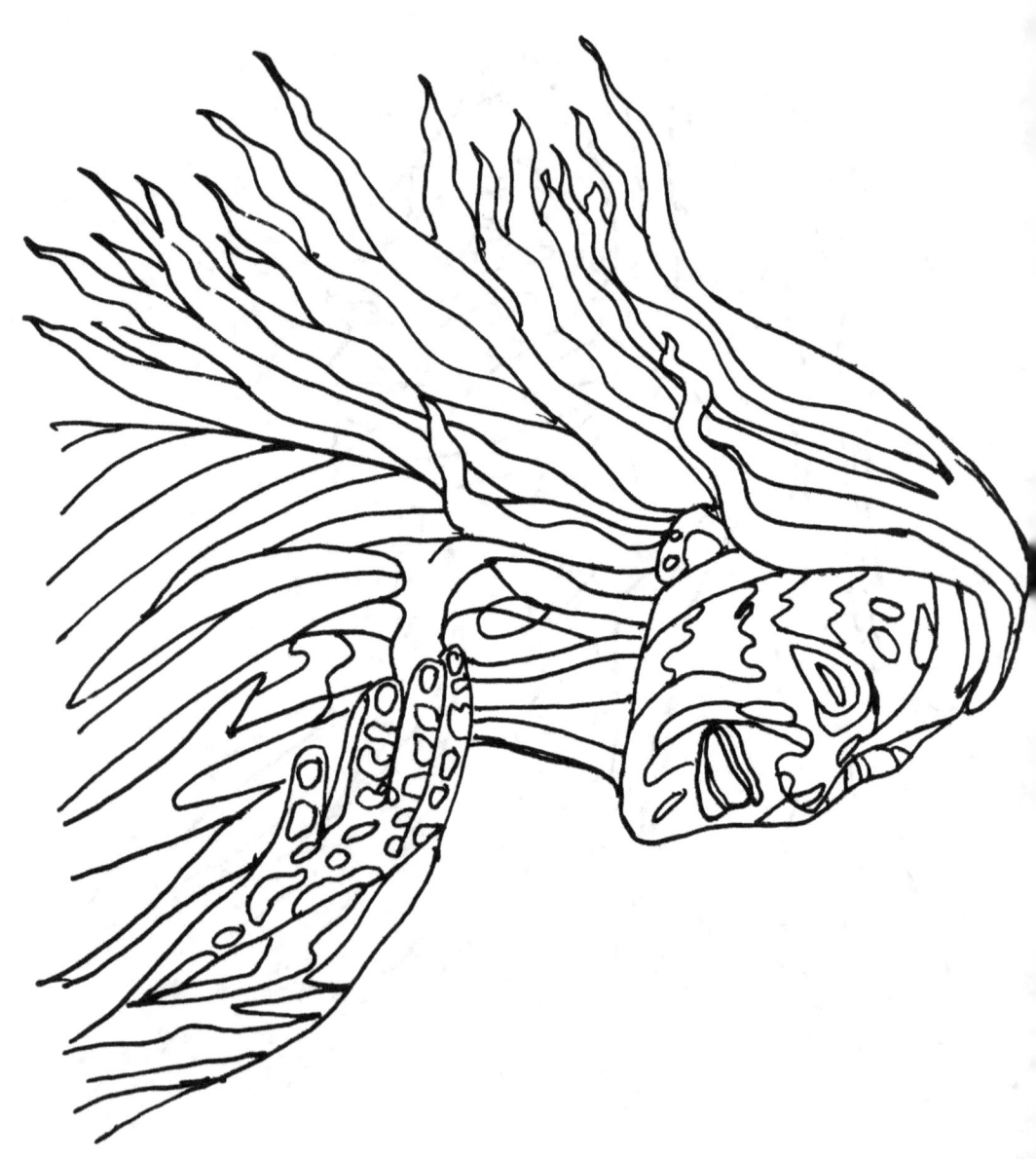

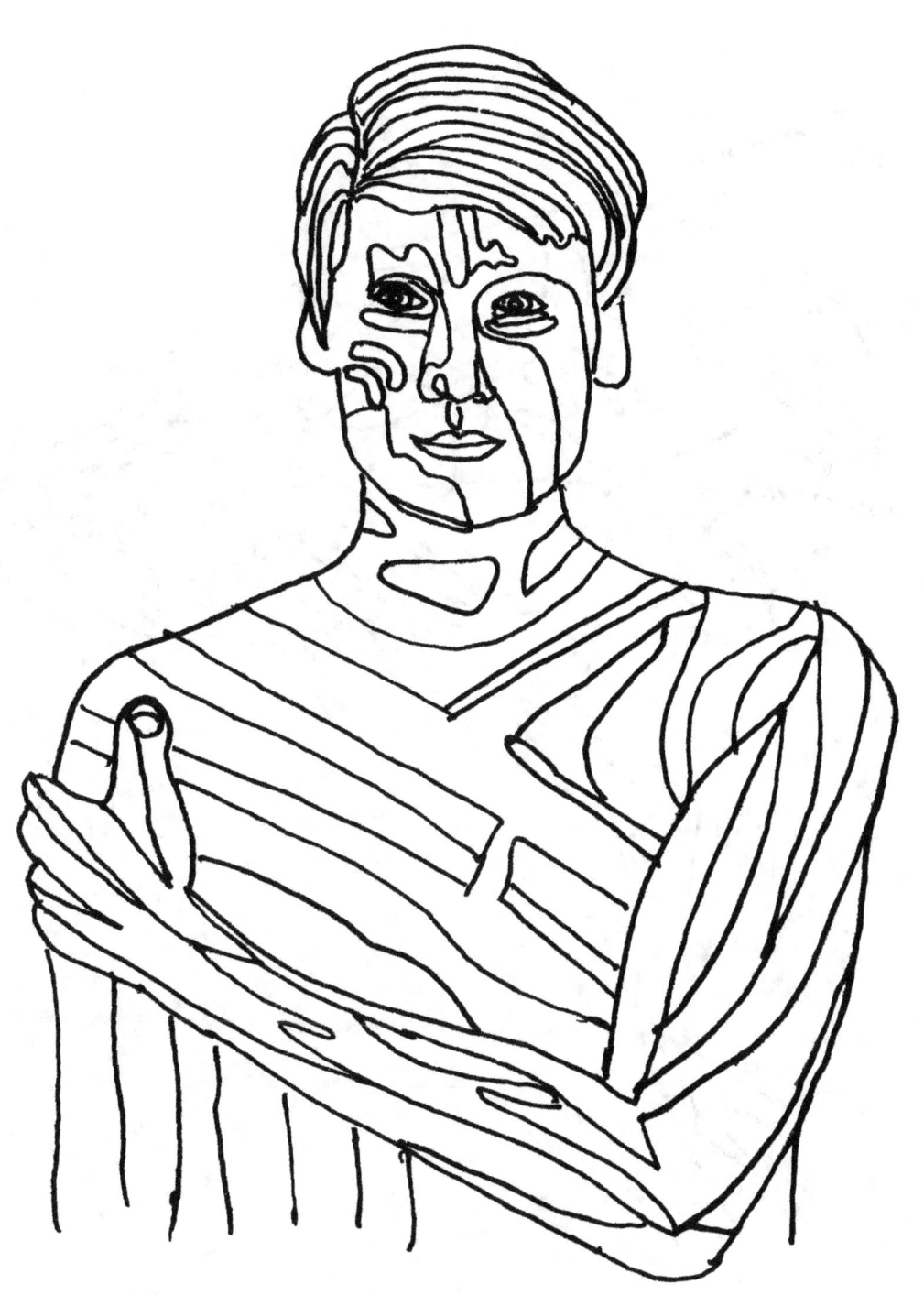

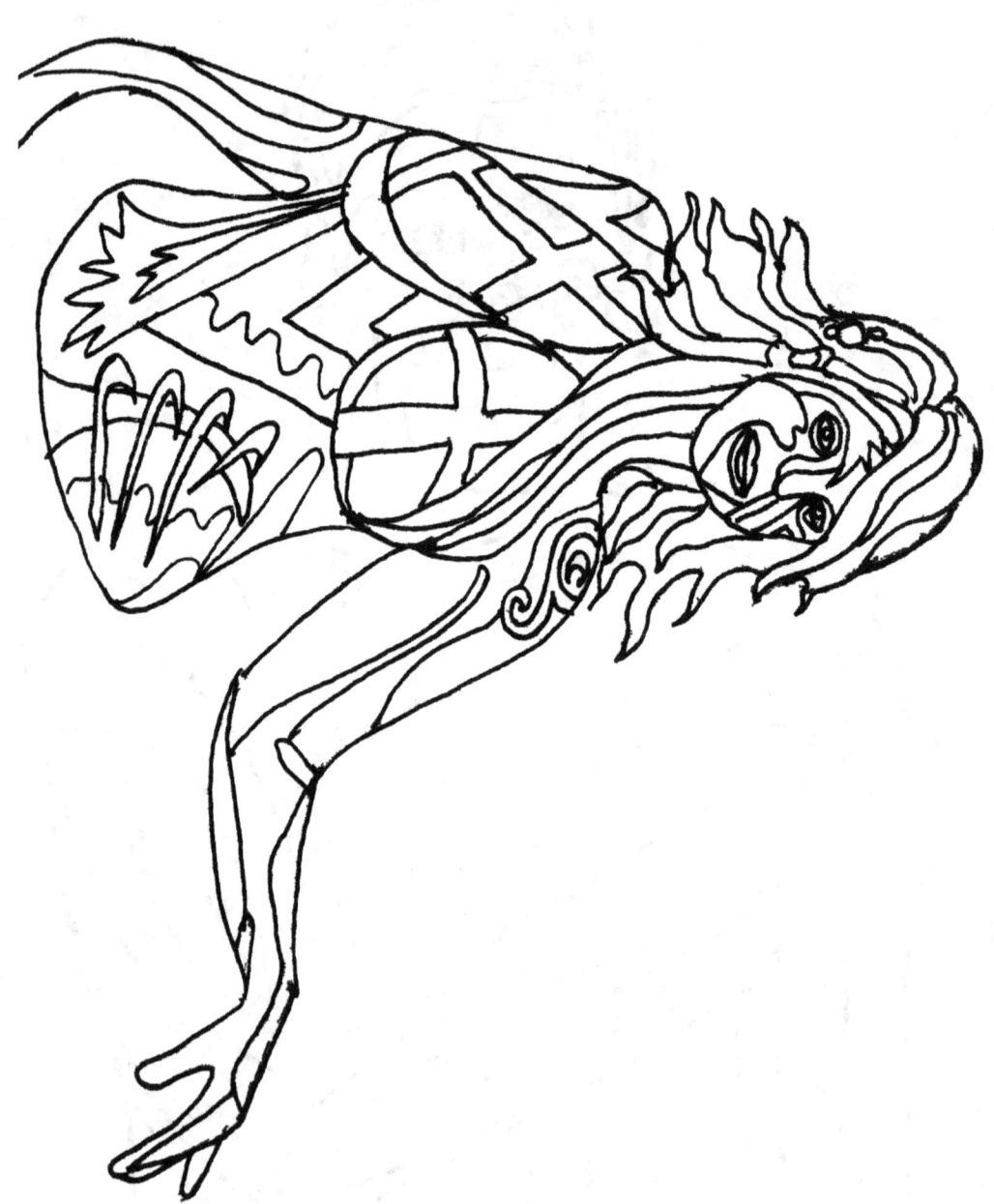

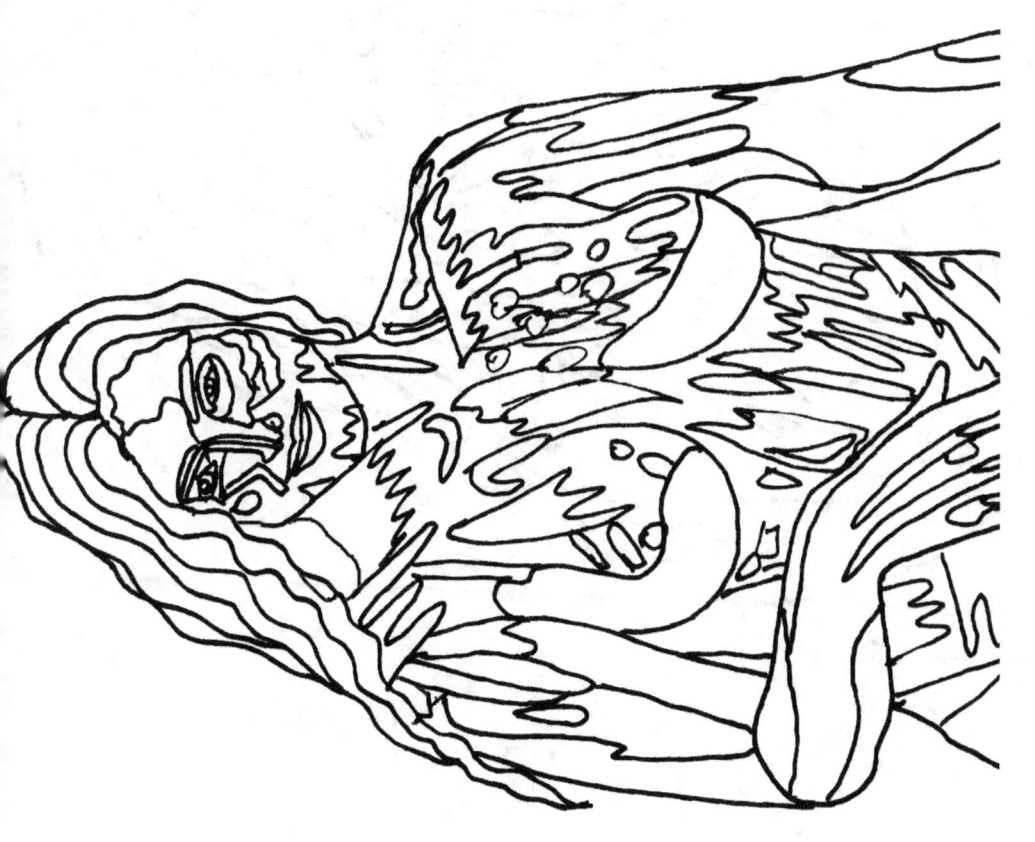

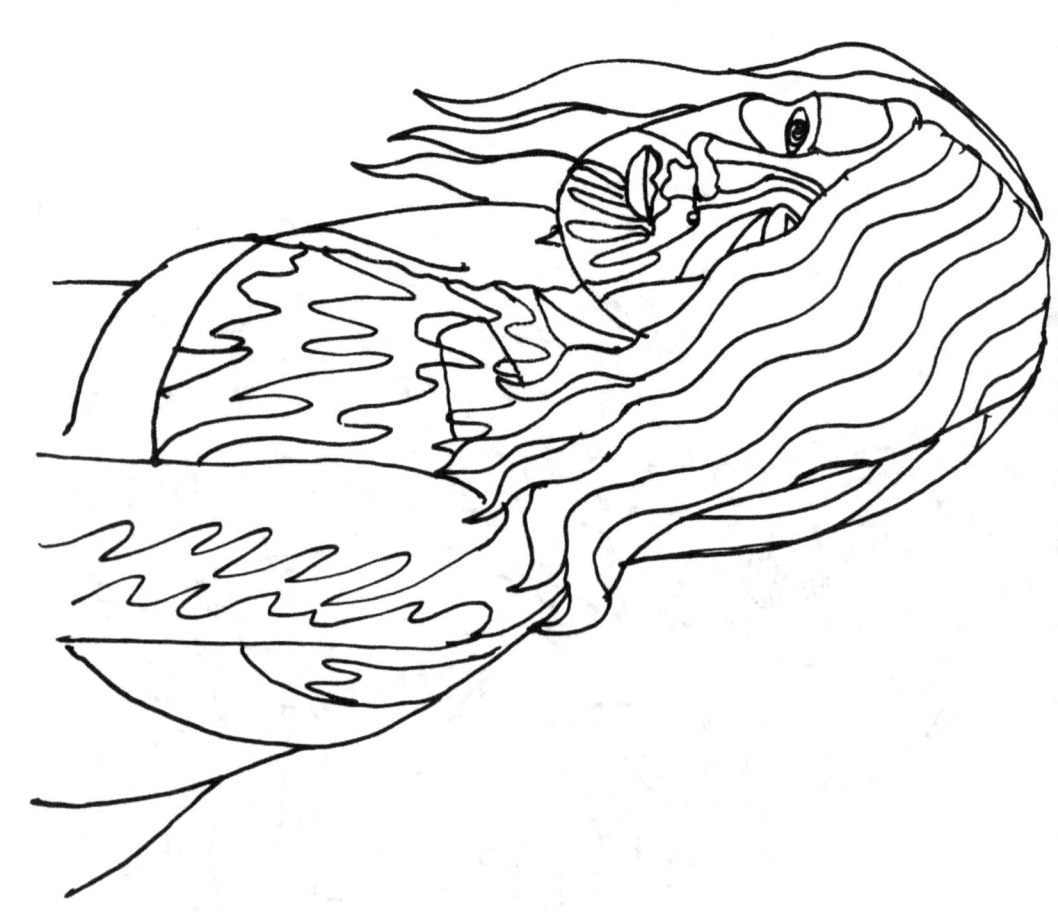

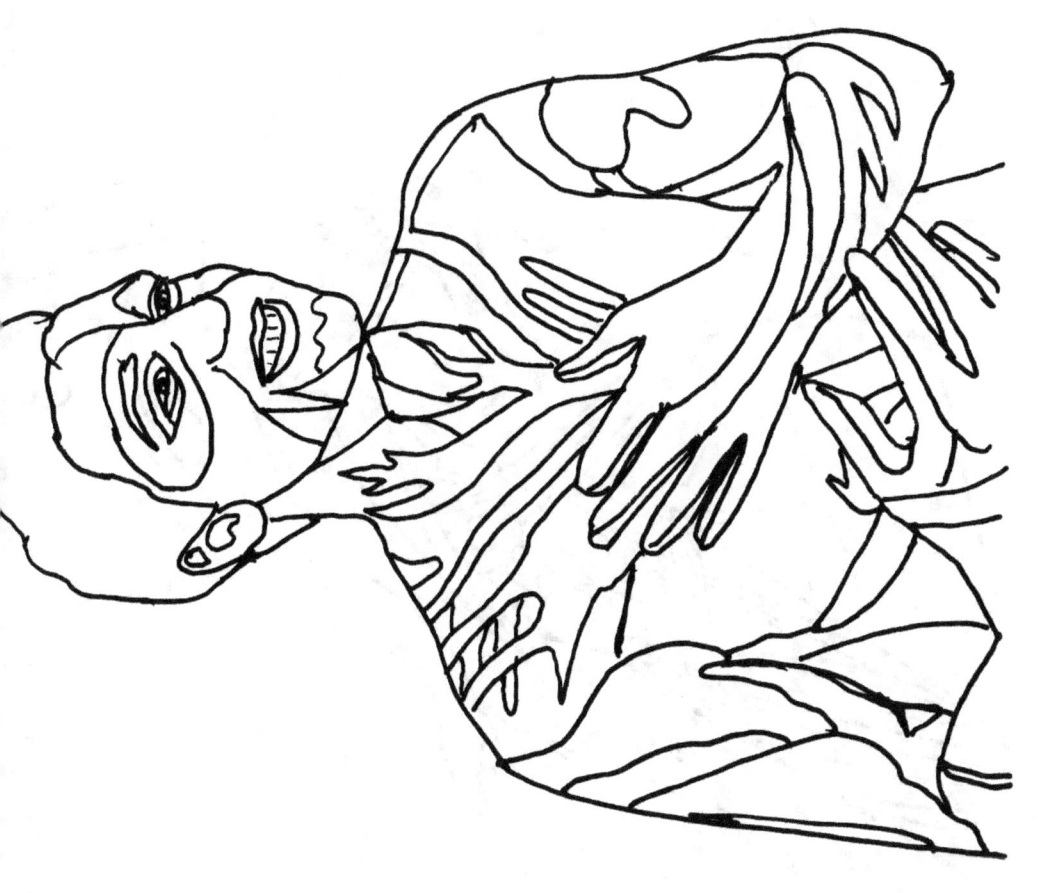

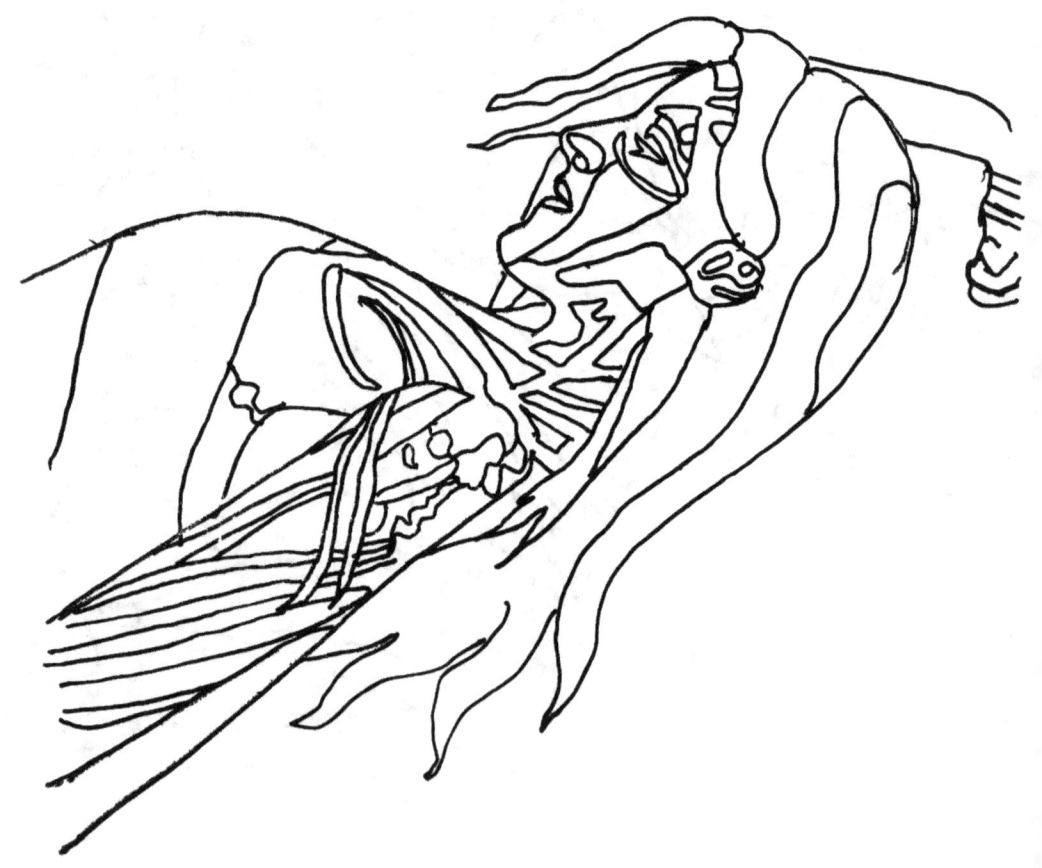

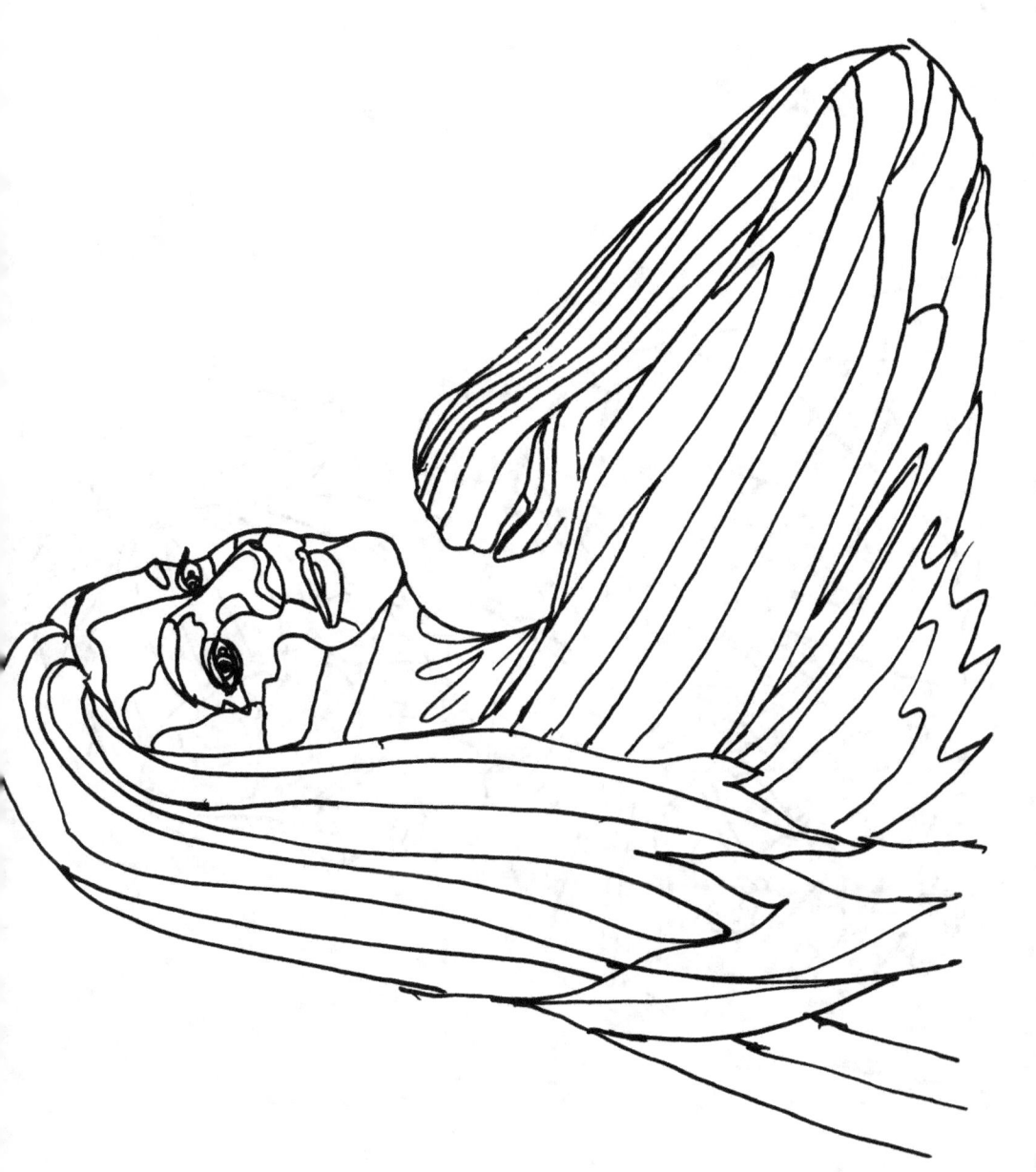

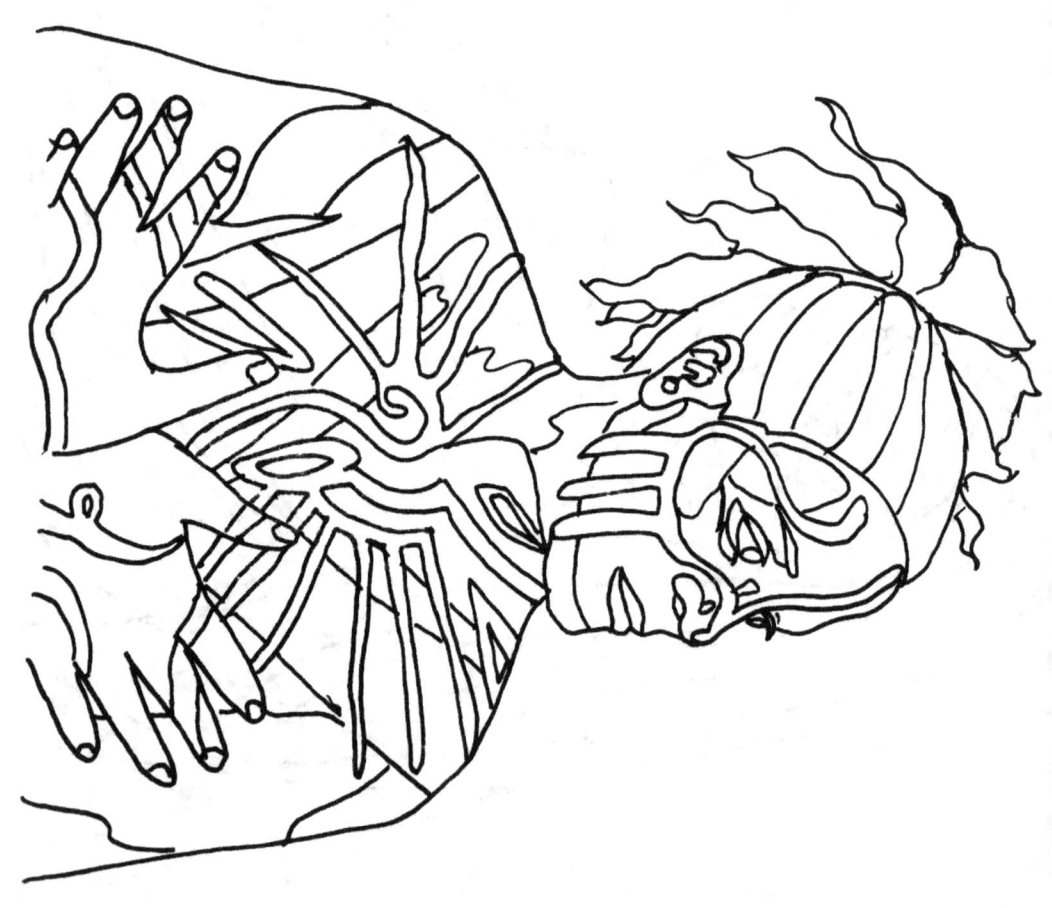

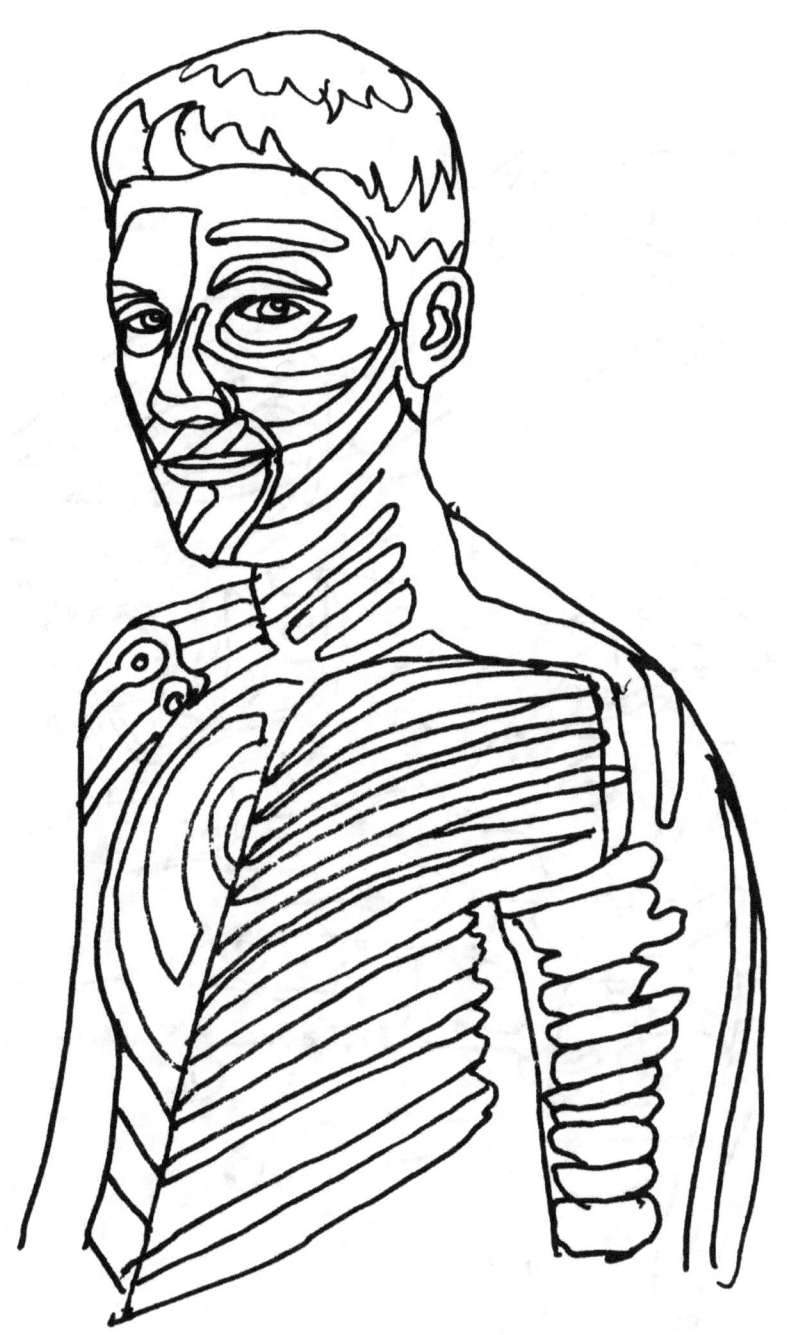

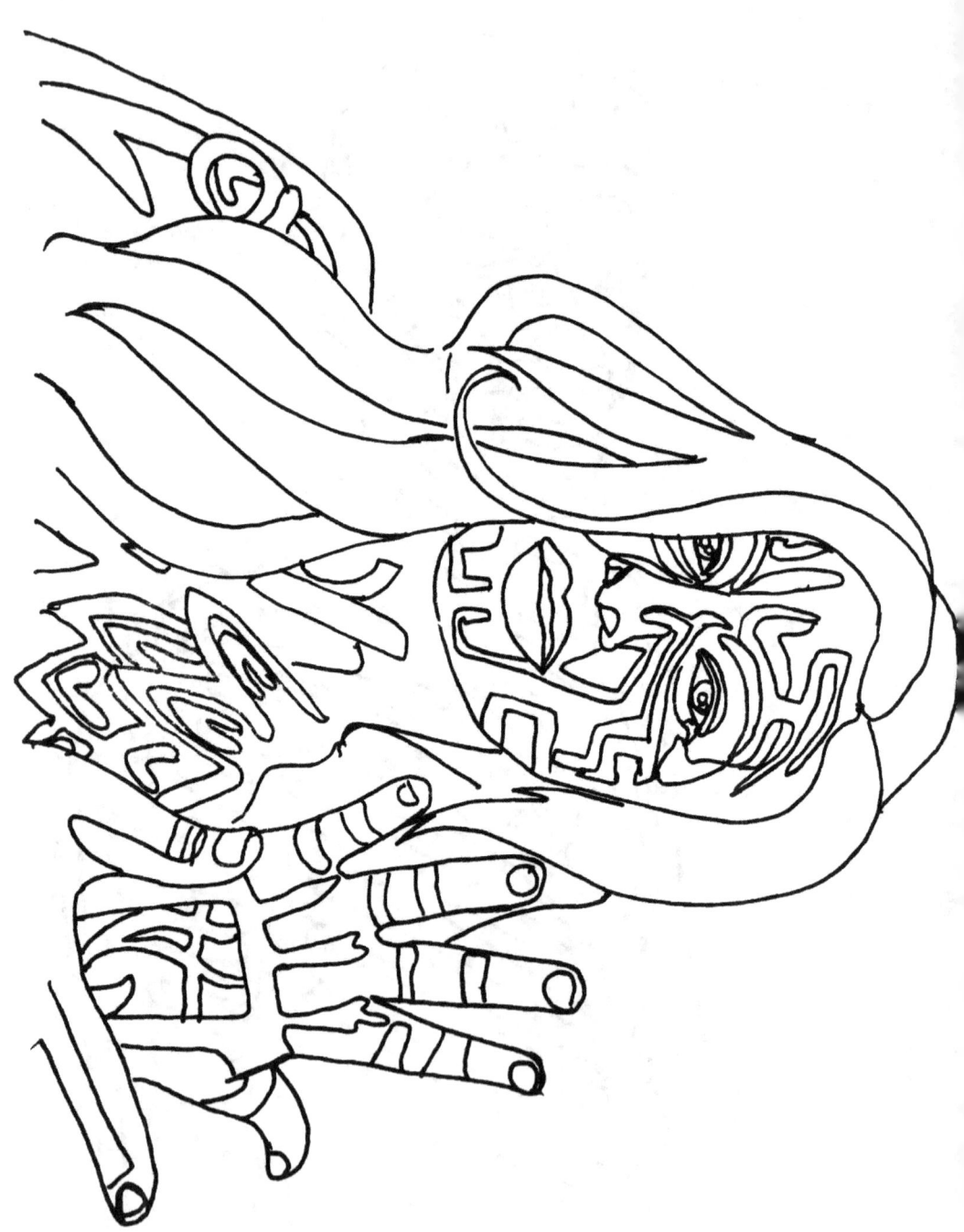